Moments with
JACKIE

Moments with
JACKIE

JEAN MILLS

MetroBooks

MetroBooks

An Imprint of Friedman/Fairfax Publishers

©1999 by Michael Friedman Publishing Group, Inc.

Library of Congress Cataloging-in-Publication Data available upon request.

ISBN 1-56799-852-6

Editor: Emily Zelner
Art Director: Jeff Batzli
Designer: Milagros Sensat
Photography Editor: Valerie E. Kennedy
Production Director: Karen Matsu Greenberg
Color separations by Colourscan Co. Pte. Ltd.
Printed in China by Leefung Asco Printers Ltd.

3 5 7 9 10 8 6 4 2

For bulk purchases and special sales, please contact:
Friedman/Fairfax Publishers
Attention: Sales Department
15 West 26th Street
New York, NY 10010
212/685-6610 FAX 212/685-1307

Visit our website:
http://www.metrobooks.com

Dedication

For Carolea and Abby

Acknowledgments

I would like to gratefully acknowledge the support and encouragement I received from the following people during the writing of this book: in Boston, my mother, Alice Jean Mills—I don't know how I got so lucky to have a mother who read to me—and my father, Stanley Robert Mills, a Jackie admirer from way back; in New York, the editors at the Michael Friedman Publishing Group, Sharyn Rosart, Ann Kirby, and Emily Zelner; my friend and agent, Susan Lee Cohen; Mt. Holyoke College's 15th reunion class of 1983, especially Margaret Murphy and Martha Holleman; and Cindy and Eric Stern, Deborah Lashley, Penny Mintz, Harry and Tova Goldfarb, Linda Katt, Kelly Ryan, Chris Lipson, and Sheilah Gersh, for their kind words and enthusiasm.

The editors would like to thank James B. Hill at the John F. Kennedy Library for all of his patience, knowledge, and consistency.

Introduction

*Throughout my life I have always tried to remain true
to myself. This I will continue to do as long as I live.*

—Jacqueline Bouvier Kennedy Onassis

WHEN ONE IS CHOSEN BY DESTINY, THE PATH AHEAD IS OFTEN fraught with challenges and complexities almost mythic in nature and size. A determination to meet those challenges and sort through the complexities is to take the high road, make order out of chaos, and find the way. Jacqueline Bouvier Kennedy Onassis conducted her life within a framework of personal dignity and integrity, which became an inspiration for people around the world.

Despite her yearnings for privacy and protection, Jackie, as we came to call her, was forced to change and grow before our eyes. By her mere presence and demeanor, she unwittingly set the standard by which generations of women felt compelled to measure themselves. Offering a fresh perspective about what made Jackie so distinctive, this tribute celebrates a woman whose importance reached beyond her sense of style, even beyond the legislative and political achievements of her first husband, John F. Kennedy, the thirty-fifth president of the United States, to transform our identities and indelibly touch our lives.

On July 28, 1929, in Southampton, New York, Jacqueline Lee Bouvier was born into a family of wealth and privilege. She grew up amid the exclusive equestrian circles of the Hamptons on Long Island, the sophisticated townhouses and private schools of New York City, and the extravagant estates of Newport, Rhode Island. Her mother, Janet Lee Bouvier, was intense and strong-willed, but instilled in her children an appreciation and respect for the arts, poetry, and languages. During her early childhood, Jackie developed a unique aesthetic sense and intellectual vibrancy that lasted a lifetime. A voracious reader, she was enjoying the short stories of Anton Chekhov by the age of six, according to family legend. She had an exquisite eye for style and an attentiveness to detail, which set her apart from other girls her age and led her to distinguish herself in drawing and writing. The arts remained a source of pleasure and relaxation for Jackie into her adulthood, and they represented a kind of intimate sanctuary she would cherish all her days.

Above: A solemn Jacqueline Kennedy attends an official function in Miami, Florida, 1963. *Opposite:* In August 1959, a young Mrs. Kennedy relaxes in Hyannis Port, Massachusetts—even in repose, she exudes an air of grace, dignity, and warmth.

Having been encouraged by her mother, who was an avid equestrienne, Jackie fell in love with horses. She competed regularly in the Hamptons' annual horse and dog shows, winning her first Blue Ribbon for horsemanship when she was five years old. Far from the "fashion queen" the media later crowned her, the adolescent Jackie was a self-avowed tomboy, who in order to become feminine, "decided to learn to dance."

Though both of Jackie's grandfathers, James T. Lee and John Vernou Bouvier, Jr., were self-made men, Grandfather Bouvier—who was known as "The Major"—alleged aristocratic beginnings and enforced traditional rules of decorum and duty, which he encouraged in his grandchildren. In her youth, Jackie spent many summers at the Major's estate, Lasata, in East Hampton, where she played with her nine cousins and her younger sister, Caroline Lee Bouvier, known as Lee. Jackie wrote and illustrated poems and stories and was an expert at inventing make-believe worlds for the other children. She was bright and creative with a flair for occasional disobedience, which was indulged by her father but frowned upon by her mother. As a grown woman, Jackie never lost her youthful vitality and persuasiveness. Her

Above: Mrs. Jacqueline Kennedy in Hyannis Port on July 14, 1960, the morning after John F. Kennedy became the Democratic nominee for president. *Opposite:* Jack and Jackie enjoy the refreshing water at Hyannis Port in the summer of 1960.

manner, sense of humor, and breathless way of speaking gave her an exceptionally engaging quality.

Jackie's father, John "Black Jack" Vernou Bouvier, III, was a stockbroker with a reputation for being loose with both women and money. He was dashing, entertaining, and well liked. Jackie was extremely close to her father. They enjoyed spending time together and their love for each other was deep and mutual. Black Jack reveled in his daughter's accomplishments and was proud of her achievements as a little girl and later as a student at boarding school and college. Despite the frequent embarrassments her father caused both her and the family in the wake of his many affairs, Jackie maintained her strong relationship with him until his death in 1957. She once compared her father's "dangerous" charisma to that of John Kennedy, and admitted that this was one of the reasons she found the young senator so attractive.

At the age of seven, Jackie's idyllic childhood world came to an end with her parents' bitter divorce. Torn between her love for her adoring father and loyalty to her mother, Jackie was forced to develop an emotional strength that would serve her well in later years. By all

accounts she missed her father terribly, and both she and her sister, Lee, suffered prolonged separations from him until the divorce was finalized in 1940. In 1942 Janet married Hugh D. Auchincloss, Jr., a wealthy stockbroker. Jackie divided her time between the Auchincloss estate, Merrywood, near Washington, D.C., and Hammersmith Farm in Newport, Rhode Island.

During her days at Hammersmith Farm, due to wartime restrictions, Jackie worked alongside her sister and newly acquired stepbrothers and stepsisters, Hugh III (Yusha), Nina, and Thomas, milking cows and feeding the chickens and livestock. Always preferring to be outside riding horses or enjoying nature, Jackie grew fond of both Merrywood and Hammersmith for the beauty, peacefulness, and security they provided her during a fractious and disruptive time in her life. Her mother's marriage also produced two other siblings, Janet junior and Jamie Auchincloss.

Jackie finished high school at Miss Porter's School in Farmington, Connecticut. At the age of seventeen, in 1947, she was named "Debutante of the Year" by Hearst gossip columnist Igor Cassini, who described her as a "regal brunette, who has classic features and the daintiness of Dresden porcelain." She studied for two years at Vassar College, spent her junior year abroad at the Sorbonne in Paris, and spent her senior year at George Washington University in Washington, D.C., where she graduated with a major in French literature. She was appreciative of the "superb teachers" she found in the areas of "all my greatest interests—in literature and art, Shakespeare and poetry." In the summer of 1951, Jackie won *Vogue*'s Prix de Paris writing contest, whose theme was "People I Wish I Had Known." She chose Sergei Diaghilev, Charles Baudelaire, and Oscar Wilde. In the contest essay—which also asked that she write about herself—Jackie reflected on what her year in Europe, away from home, had taught her. She wrote, "I learned not to be ashamed of a real hunger for knowledge, something I had always tried to hide."

After college, Jackie took a job with the now defunct *Washington Times-Herald* in December 1951, writing a regular column called "The Inquiring Camera Girl." It was her job to come up with amusing questions to ask the people she met in and around Washington, D.C. The questions and their equally amusing answers appeared alongside the interviewee's photograph. One of her subjects was a young senator from Massachusetts, John F. Kennedy.

and prestige. Jack was proud of Jackie's accomplishments and her deep knowledge of history and the arts. He once told a friend that when Jackie spoke French (which she did fluently), he could understand only one in five words she said—and that was "de Gaulle." She was tall, strikingly lovely, with an easy elegance and impeccable taste, sophisticated, but intriguing and dignified. Jackie attended Eisenhower's inaugural ball in January 1953 with Jack as her escort. On June 23, 1953, she announced her engagement to John Kennedy to the public.

Jackie was in love with Jack. She discovered that they shared an

Jackie first met John Kennedy at a party in Washington, D.C., in May 1951. She later became engaged to another man, John Husted, in December 1951. But when she met Kennedy again, they began dating, and Jackie called off her engagement to Husted in March 1952. During the summer of that year she was introduced to the Irish energy and ambition of the entire Kennedy clan, about which she remarked, "Just watching them wore me out." But she found the Kennedys and their ways stimulating, upbeat, and open, in direct contrast to the more introspective, reserved lifestyle of the Auchinclosses.

To Jack Kennedy, Jackie had a distinctive air. She was bright and beautiful, possessing a graceful, clever ability to play down her attributes

undefinable chemistry that would keep them together through both difficult and happy times. She also found that they shared a regard for privacy and the dignity that comes from respecting that privacy. Despite the fact that both their lives were subject to intense public interest, they managed to reserve part of themselves for just each other.

While Jackie's mother, Janet, was less than enthusiastic about the couple's union, Jack's father, Joseph Kennedy, adored Jackie and was well aware of the class and social status she brought to the Kennedy image. Jack and Jackie's marriage on September 12, 1953, became an extremely important social occasion, dubbed by the media "The Wedding of the Year."

A year after the wedding Jack nearly died after undergoing spinal surgery. Jackie cared for Jack and took charge of all of his political correspondence and communication while he recovered. Though she was devoted to her husband, it took time for Jackie to adjust to the rigors of his campaign life and she grew slowly into her role as ideal political wife. She did not like campaigning because the constant traveling prevented them from having a proper home and later took her away from her children. Jackie yearned for stability and roots, and what she longed for most was a home and children. Though she eventually found campaigning rewarding, initially she felt grossly unprepared for the toll it took on her marriage.

After a few months on the campaign trail, however, Jackie and Jack's skeptical advisors realized that the people loved her. Behind the elegance and seemingly cool, royal exterior was a woman who was truly fascinated by people. She genuinely loved to hear their stories. Rather than being turned off by her sophisticated elegance, as Jack's political "experts" had suspected, people reveled in her charms and enjoyed her sense of humor and intelligence. Jackie's natural form of diplomacy personified grace and style. Her influence on the public surprised Jackie most of all, but it gave her confidence, too. She discovered she had a talent for creating unique worlds and setting trends.

Jack and Jackie became the golden couple who stood at the center of the American political and cultural climates of the decade. But despite the couple's elevation in the eyes of the press, their relationship, like all relationships, had its share of difficulties. The first year of their marriage Jackie was alone almost every weekend. Sometimes during Jack's

Above: Between engagements, Jack and Jackie are caught in a moment of laughter as they leave Blair House and look forward to attending the arrival ceremonies for the president of Tunisia on May 3, 1961. Opposite: Jackie was a devout Roman Catholic and attended mass frequently; here she is seen entering St. Edward's Roman Catholic Church in Palm Beach Florida, on December 24, 1961.

Above: Jackie often worried about the effect the demands of the White House had on her children. Here, Jackie and daughter Caroline cuddle in the window seat of their winter residence in Palm Beach, Florida, on February 13, 1961. *Opposite:* John, Jr., playfully pulls at his mother's pearl necklace in this famous photo taken in 1962 by official White House photographer Cecil Stoughton.

political campaigns she was on her own for weeks at a time. The couple did not have their own home until 1957, when their eldest child, Caroline, was three weeks old. By the time Caroline was born, on November 27 of that year, Jackie had already experienced two failed pregnancies, one in October 1955, which ended in miscarriage, and one in August 1956, which ended with the baby being stillborn. Caroline was born prematurely but healthy, and John F. Kennedy, Jr., would be born on November 25, 1960, just weeks after Jack's election to office. Another son, Patrick Bouvier Kennedy, would be born five weeks early on August 7, 1963, but died at only three days old.

Still, in spite of the strains brought on by the grueling pace of a political, high-profile family, Jackie kept Jack as her main priority. She loved him and she believed in his vision. She enjoyed Jack's speeches and accurately viewed him as a natural speechmaker who exerted a powerful impact on an audience. He, in turn, was grateful for her assistance in helping him to prepare by giving him literary allusions and quotes appropriate for any given issue. Jackie, too, gave speeches. With humor and grace, she defended her husband's religion against anti-Catholic sentiment, an action that was instrumental in his ultimate success in the election.

When Jack Kennedy was campaigning for the presidency in 1960, Jackie was pregnant with John, Jr. Unable to travel during much of the campaign, she wrote a syndicated column called "The Campaign Wife." John F. Kennedy was elected president of the United States in November 1960. Barely one month before Inauguration Day in January 1961, Jackie gave birth to John, Jr. When a reporter asked what kind of concessions she would be making in her new role as First Lady, Jackie quipped, "I will wear hats." But behind her humor was a certain degree of fear and anxiety about raising her children in full view of a relentless public eye. She once remarked about her life in the White House, "My first fight was to fight for a sane life for my babies and their father." Jackie's desire for privacy within the parameters of courtesy and protocol were legendary.

Nowhere were these two opposing philosophies so skillfully joined than in Jackie's restoration of the White House. On the one hand, she said she never wanted to live in "a house where you have to say to the children 'Don't touch!'" But she also believed that the White House belonged to the nation and should inspire people and make Americans proud of their heritage. When Jackie first moved into the White House, she was appalled at the condition and maintenance of what was supposed to be part of the "best" America had to offer. As First Lady, Jackie made restoring the White House one of her main objectives. Like Jack, Jackie had a great respect for history and the ability to learn from the past. She researched White House history and restored the entire building and grounds for the nation to appreciate. In order to continue the upkeep of the White House for succeeding administrations and future generations of young people, she established the White House Historical Association and began publication of a White House guidebook. Since 1961, the guidebook has sold about 8 million copies, with all proceeds benefiting the historical preservation of the White House.

Together, Jackie and Jack expressed the values of twentieth-century America, but their influence was actually worldwide. With the remodeling of the White House and the first party at the White House for Nobel Prize winners, which Jackie organized in April 1962, she encouraged an awareness of the cultural and historical traditions of the nation.

There are reasons beyond circumstances why one becomes a beloved cultural icon. Both Jackie and Jack shared an appreciation of intellectual accomplishment. Many of the same superlatives attributed to John F. Kennedy could be used to describe Jackie. She was a woman of uncommon courage, endurance, independence, wit, intelligence, charisma, beauty, and grace. But what became clear to the world was that Jackie could create an atmosphere merely by entering the room. Her presence at an event was a challenge for others to excel.

As it was for the world, the assassination of John F. Kennedy was a defining, life-altering event. For all of us, but for no one more than Jackie, the violence of Jack's death was accompanied by fear,

The smile returns to Jackie's face as she is photographed in Greece during a trip that was meant to revitalize her spirits after the death of her third child, Patrick Bouvier Kennedy.

humiliation, degradation, violation, bitterness, and shame. On November 22, 1963, in Dallas, Texas, Jackie was seated beside Jack in the presidential motorcade when the assassin's bullets, cheating destiny, took the president's life. One never fully recovers from such a loss, and she never really did, but Jackie chose to persevere. Handling so public a tragedy with dignity, integrity, and courage, Jackie stood beside Vice President Lyndon Johnson as he was sworn in aboard Air Force One as the next president of the United States. She refused to change out of her suit, which was stained with the blood of her husband. Returning to Washington, D.C., she personally saw to it that her husband was properly honored, making the funeral arrangements based on Abraham Lincoln's funeral. She insisted that there be no undertakers and that everything be handled by the U.S. Navy, in which Jack had served. It was Jackie's idea to march to St. Matthew's Cathedral come rain or shine. Jackie also sent word down that Jack was to be buried at Arlington National Cemetery instead of Hyannis Port for, as she once told him, "You just belong to all the country." Before the funeral, she wrote Jack a good-bye letter. Caroline also wrote a letter, and John, Jr., too young to write, scribbled a note to his father as well. Jackie had all three notes buried with Jack inside the coffin.

As events swirled about her, Jackie was a pillar of strength. The quiet strength she displayed at Jack's funeral inspired the nation and won the admiration of the world. From that day on, she took hold of our hearts and never let go. Drawing on the wellspring of her emotional resiliency, she taught the world how to mourn. Shouldering the responsibilities of a nation hungry for stability and inclusion, she showed us that we could rise from our knees together, raise our faces, and together begin to rebuild. We saw that if she were somehow able to recover a sense of purpose in life, then certainly we could. But what few of us knew was that Jackie presented a brave face to the world at great personal sacrifice

to herself, including bouts of loneliness and deep despair. A year later, she wrote an essay in honor of Jack, which appeared in the November 27, 1964, issue of *Look* magazine. Her profound grief was evident when she wrote:

> *I don't think there is any consolation. What was lost cannot be replaced. . . . Now I think I should have known that he was magic all along. I did know it—but I should have guessed it could not last. I should have known that it was asking too much to dream that I might have grown old with him and see our children grow up together. . . . I think for him—at least he will never know whatever sadness might have lain ahead. He knew such a share of it in his life that it always made you so happy whenever you saw him enjoying himself. But now he will never know more. . . . He is free and we must live.*

After tragedy, the challenge is to discover meaning, to find a way to put chaos and random acts into perspective. It is difficult to rekindle a desire to continue or find a love of life when the flame has been so violently extinguished before one's eyes. Jackie would have preferred the nation to remember Jack's birthday rather than the infamous day of his death. But that was not to be. After the assassination, Jackie moved her family to Georgetown, but in the autumn of 1964 she moved to New York City and bought an apartment on Fifth Avenue. She didn't begin to appear at public and social occasions again until 1966.

With Jack's death, Jackie found her strength and inspiration in her duty and responsibility to her children. As a mother, she realized that there was no greater way to face the future than by raising her children well. The public had always known that Jackie was there for her children, watching them, applauding their accomplishments, and just letting them know that she loved them. Jackie's move to New York City was an effort to extricate her children from the political pressures of Washington, D.C., and to protect them from the realities of violence she rightly feared.

Jackie believed strongly that children, especially children growing up in the public eye, need personal attention and support from their parents.

In New York City she strove to create as normal a life as possible for Caroline and John Jr., even though she and the children were under intense public scrutiny every day. Nothing meant more to Jackie than her family. She once said about motherhood, "I've seen the worst of everything. I've seen the best of everything. But I can't replace my family."

After the assassination, Jackie became extremely close to Jack's brother Robert F. Kennedy, relying on him for advice and a kind of fatherly presence for her children. When Bobby was assassinated during his bid for the presidency in 1968, Jackie became more fearful,

Above: In May, 1990, Jackie proudly attended a dedication and unveiling ceremony of a statue of President John F. Kennedy for the Massachusetts State-house lawn in Boston. Opposite: Jackie and Maurice Tempelsman greeting President Bill Clinton and Mrs. Clinton aboard the Relemar in Martha's Vineyard, Massachusetts, in August, 1993.

understanding how she could marry a man who was seemingly the antithesis of her first husband, the young, charismatic Jack Kennedy. Jackie's marriage to Ari Onassis was a bold act, given the fact that her golden image was entwined with the Kennedy name and entrenched in the American people's imagination.

By the autumn of 1973, the Onassis marriage had become strained from outside pressures and long periods of separation. On March 15, 1975, Aristotle Onassis died of pneumonia. In Athens after his funeral, Jackie said, "Aristotle Onassis rescued me at a time when my life was engulfed in shadows. He

private, and protective than ever before. Understandably, she grew terrified of living any longer in the United States, where she feared her children could become targets of violence. Relinquishing her public persona as the dignified "Kennedy widow" and seeking first and foremost to protect her children, Jackie fled the country. In October 1968, a few short months after the deaths of both Martin Luther King, Jr., and Bobby Kennedy, Jackie married Greek shipping tycoon Aristotle Onassis on the Greek island of Skorpios. She had first met Onassis, a man several years her senior, during her recovery from the loss of her son Patrick in 1963.

During her marriage to Onassis, Jackie and her children had twenty-four-hour security. The American public had a difficult time

meant a lot to me. He brought me into a world where one could find both happiness and love. We lived through many beautiful experiences together which cannot be forgotten, and for which I will be eternally grateful."

Upon returning to New York City in the early 1970s, Jackie became involved in the fight to save Grand Central Station and together with the city's Municipal Art Society fought against the Columbus Circle building that would have been the tallest building in the world. Happy to have her back home, the press renewed its quest for "Jackie O" and followed her wherever she went. One of her more well-known friends at the time, Mike Nichols, once said that escorting Jackie anywhere was "like going out with a national monument."

In the fall of 1975, Jackie accepted a job as an editor at Viking Press. Despite her impeccable record and qualifications, she often found that she had to defend herself against attacks on her professionalism. She quite accurately explained when she was questioned as to whether or not she had earned her position in publishing: "It's not as if I've never done anything interesting. I've been a reporter myself and I've lived through important parts of American history. I'm not the worst choice for the position." In 1977, she felt compelled to resign over Jeffrey Archer's novel *Shall We Tell the President?* which portrayed Ted Kennedy as the focus of an assassination plot. In spring 1978, Jackie moved on to become an editor at Doubleday, where she specialized in nonfiction books.

In 1988, Jackie found she had a great deal in common with a man who had been friendly with the Kennedys in the 1950s. Belgian-born financier Maurice Tempelsman shared Jackie's passion for art and antiques, and together they enjoyed walks in Central Park, birding, and sailing. Jackie feared that her fame, manifest in the relentless pursuit of her by paparazzi, might prove too great an obstacle to a relationship, but Maurice handled the invasion of privacy with a dignity that matched her own, and he was her devoted companion for seven years.

Jacqueline Bouvier Kennedy Onassis succumbed to non-Hodgkins lymphoma on May 19, 1994. Four days later she was laid to rest alongside John F. Kennedy at Arlington National Cemetery. Her death saddened millions, not just in America, but around the world, a measure of the regard in which she was held. Jackie herself was entirely modest about her achievements. But we remember and admire Jackie in all her roles—as a young woman eager for knowledge, devoted wife and mother, First Lady, preservationist, and respected editor. To each of these vocations, she brought her characteristic blend of style and quiet determination. Most of all, she will be remembered for her example of a life lived with courage, respect, and dignity—this will prove Jackie's enduring legacy.

Moments with Jackie

Above: Jackie, the little equestrienne, sits astride her pony, Buddy, being led by her adoring father, John "Black Jack" Vernou Bouvier, III, in Southampton, New York, on August 11, 1934. *Opposite:* Six-year-old Jackie, left, and her three-year-old sister, Lee, pose with their dog, Regent, at the annual dog show in East Hampton, New York, in 1935.

Opposite: Jackie, by now an accomplished equestrienne, looks on with an air of determination at the 1941 East Hampton horse show on Long Island.
Below: A young Jackie Bouvier with her dog, Tammy, awaits the annual dog show at the East Hampton Fair on July 28, 1939.

Opposite: Seen here posing for her wedding portrait, Jackie is the picture of elegance. *Below:* "The Wedding of the Year." Twenty-four-year-old Jacqueline Lee Bouvier marries John F. Kennedy, then a United States senator from Massachusetts, at St. Mary's Church in Newport, Rhode Island, on September 12, 1953.

Jackie's new father-in-law, Joseph P. Kennedy, kisses the radiant bride as Senator John F. Kennedy looks on at their reception in Newport, Rhode Island, on September 12, 1953.

Above: Jackie and Jack—the couple that would capture the hearts of the people—cut their wedding cake as John's younger brother Robert Kennedy cheers them on.

An adventurous couple, Jack and Jackie (pictured here on their honeymoon, out for a sail with a friend) spent many happy hours at sea. During their honeymoon, Jackie even wrote a poem for Jack that ended with the lines, "And all that waits for him / Is the sea and the wind." *Pages 30–31:* Jackie and Jack entertain guests, including brother-in-law Bobby and Ethel Kennedy, in June 1957 at their new Georgetown town house. Jackie loved their new residence, which they moved into when daughter Caroline was only three weeks old.

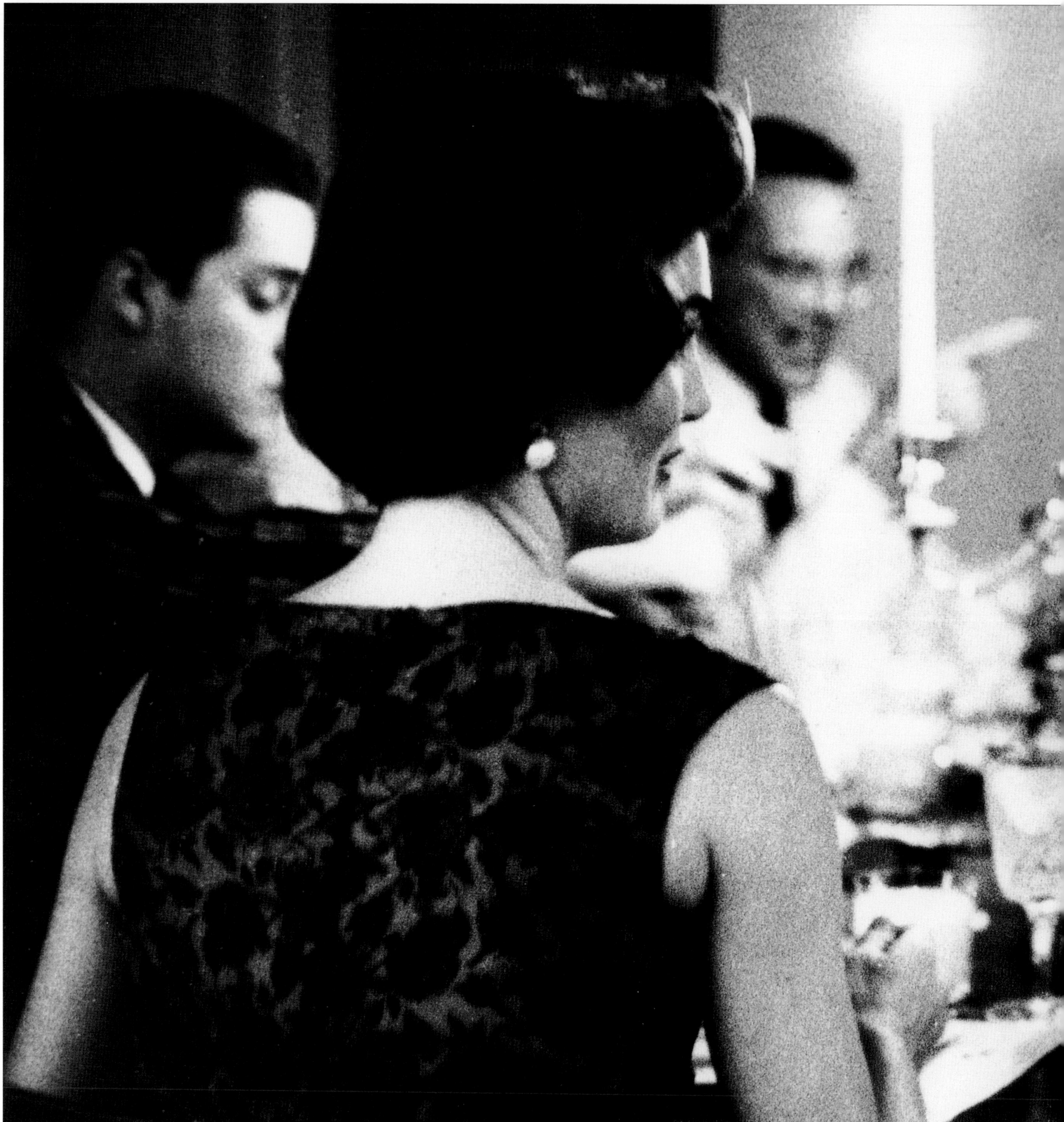

Jack and Jackie took every opportunity to be together and to spend time with their children. Their genuine enjoyment of these few moments is evident in these photographs taken in August 1959. Sharing such moments with the world was part of the magic that made people love them. Above: Caroline enjoys being held up in her father's arms while Jackie lovingly watches her husband and daughter. Opposite: Jackie holds Caroline as she says good-bye to Jack in August 1959. Jackie found it difficult to adjust to Jack's frequent absences from home during his political campaigning, and cherished the times when they were all together.

34 *Jackie takes a break from the boisterous company of the Kennedys at their summer residence in Hyannis Port in August 1959.*

Jackie had no desire to influence fashion or politics. Her highest priority was spending time with Jack and her children. Here, she passes on her love of books to two-year-old daughter Caroline.

Below: Caroline gives her father a kiss on the cheek as Jackie looks on during their summer at Hyannis Port in 1960.

Above: Jackie, pregnant here with her second child, John, Jr., shares a laugh with Caroline in August 1960.

Below: Caroline grew accustomed to the camera at a young age. Here Caroline, age two, sits on her mother's lap with her father proudly looking on while a photographer captures the family on film. Years later, Jackie said, "It's the best thing I've ever done. Being a mother is what I think has made me the person I am."

Above: An animal-lover since she was a little girl, Jackie shared this love with her family. Pictured here, Jackie holds the family cat while Jack carries Caroline during a family stroll at Hyannis Port in July 1960, before Jack leaves to hit the campaign trail.

Despite her desire to remain in the background of the Washington political scene, Mrs. Kennedy eventually became the quintessential First Lady, who met her duties with style and authority. But Jackie's contributions were evident well before she and Jack moved into the White House. Jackie took great care in decorating their first home in Georgetown and made a very conscious effort to make their home a place where they could relax and retreat from the busy political scene.

39

Jack and Jackie share a private joke during a $100-a-plate dinner at a Democratic fund-raiser on September 20, 1960. It was at this event that Jack made his first nationally televised speech.

Aboard Kennedy's private plane, the Caroline, *Jackie puts her feet up and relaxes with a copy of Jack Kerouac's* On the Road *in the spring of 1960. Jackie's taste in literature was wide-ranging; her intellectual curiosity never flagged.*

Opposite: Jack and Jackie parade down New York City's Canyon of Heroes in a ticker tape parade during Jack's 1960 run for president. Crowds lined the streets to catch a glimpse of the couple who had captured their hearts. *Below:* Jack Kennedy, the Democratic presidential nominee, and Jackie attend the Columbus Day parade on Fifth Avenue in New York City, 1960. Whether Jack was campaigning for the senatorial or presidential race, Jackie was always by his side.

44

The newly crowned king and queen of Camelot attend the festivities on Inauguration Day, January 1961, by chauffeur-driven limousine.

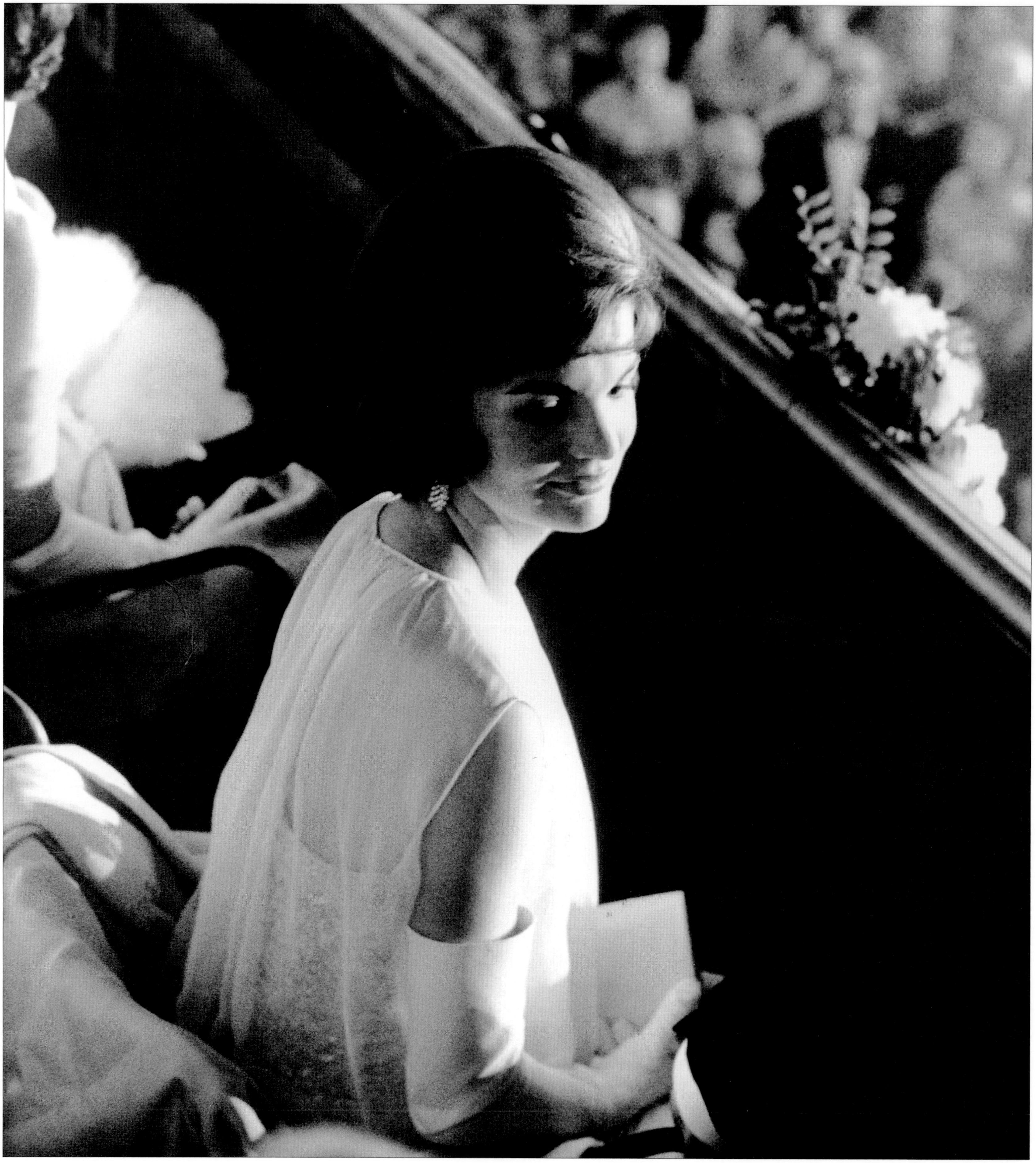

Opposite: The First Lady is the picture of style and grace seated in the presidential box during the Inaugural Ball on January 20, 1961. *Above:* The First Lady chats casually with Vice President Lyndon B. Johnson in the presidential box at the National Guard Armory during Inaugural Ball festivities.

Pages 50-51: Poised and demure, Mrs. Kennedy is seated in the Diplomatic Reception Room of the White House. She is about to appear for the first time on television in a personal salute to the National Gallery in Washington, D.C., March 1961. Opposite: Jackie returns to France as First Lady with Jack in June 1961. The now-famous trip to Paris was a phenomenal success with Jackie unwittingly taking center stage. Jack took great pride in Jackie's warm and enthusiastic reception in France. He quipped, "I am the man who accompanied Jacqueline Kennedy to Paris—and I have enjoyed it." Pictured here are Jack and Jackie with Mrs. James Gavin, the wife of the U.S. ambassador to France.

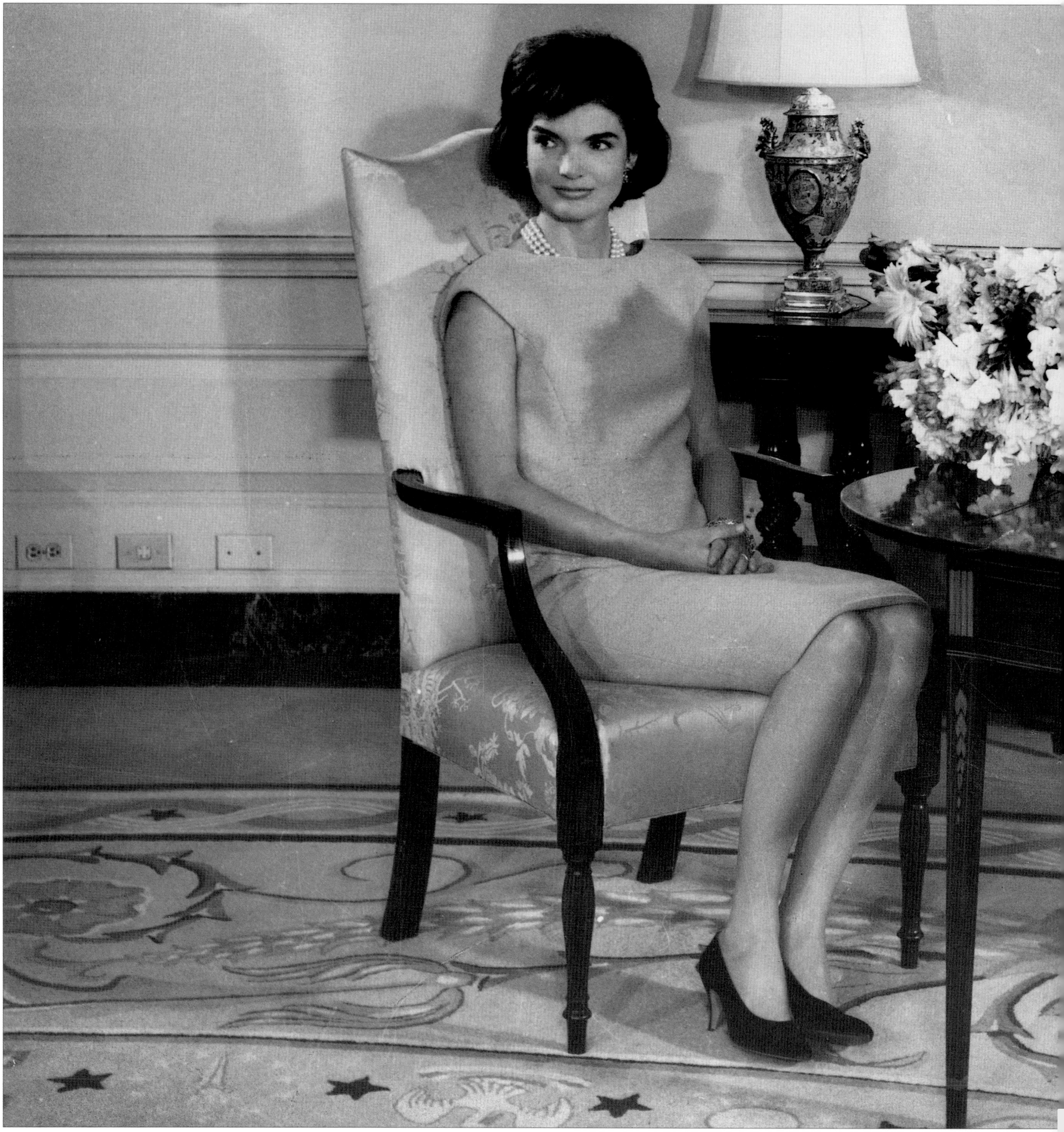

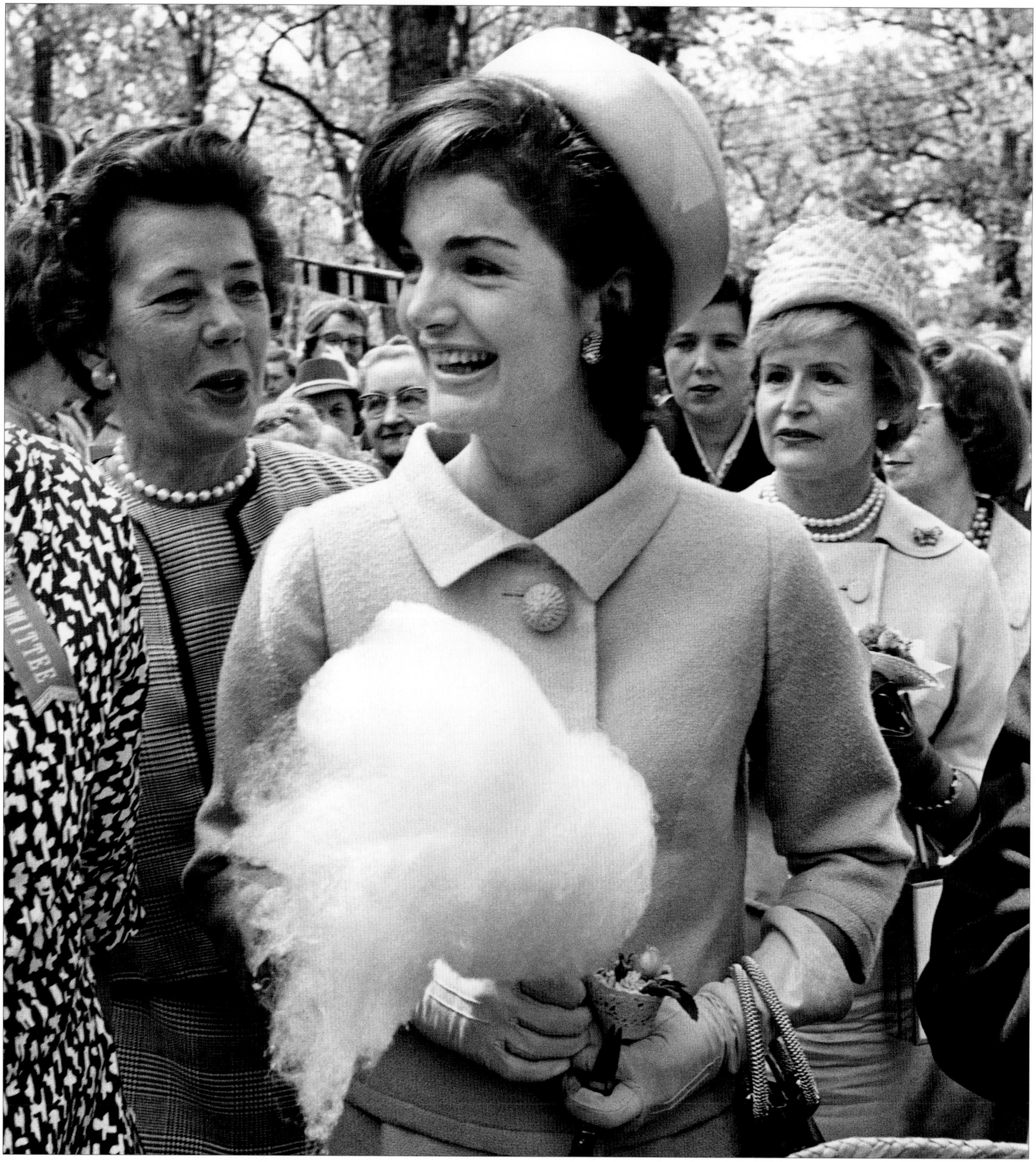

Opposite: Jackie was equally comfortable with heads of state and ladies who lunch, and her duties took her into both worlds. Here she is seen holding cotton candy and a pair of scissors that she used to cut the ribbon at the opening of the Annual Flower Mart at Washington Cathedral on May 5, 1961. The funds raised were to be used for plantings and maintenance of the cathedral grounds. *Below:* Jack tenderly adjusts Jackie's wind-blown hair and they smile at each other affectionately, as they leave Blair House for the White House after having met with the president of Tunisia in May 1961.

Above: The First Lady consults the Peruvian president's wife while President Kennedy greets President Prado during a visit to South America in September 1961.

Opposite: Despite her often cool exterior, Jackie had a natural gift for connecting with people from all walks of life. Here, she shares a laugh with a woman while on a walking tour of a South American village.

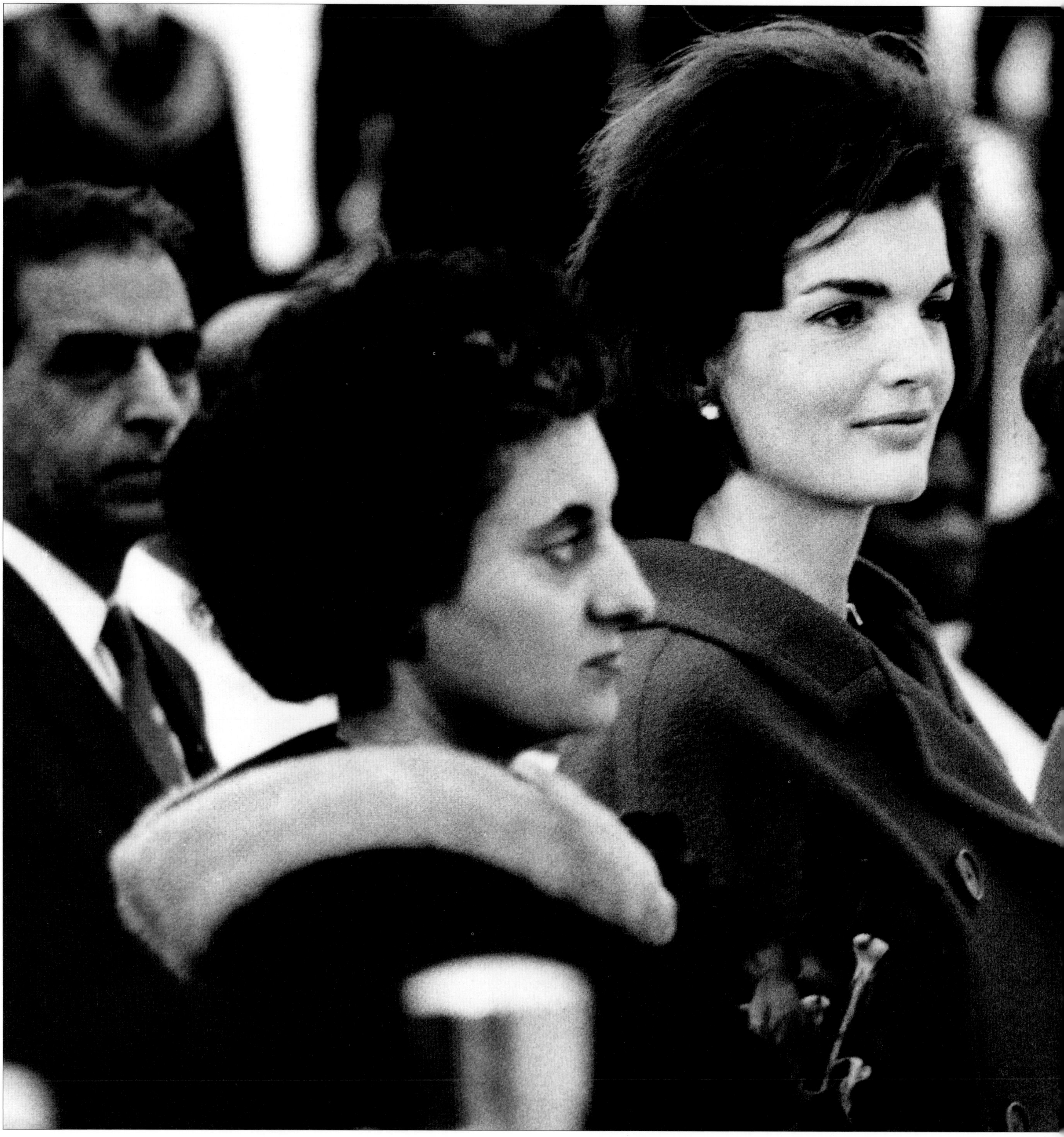

A row of remarkable women: Jackie sits with Indira Ghandi and Lady Bird Johnson during the visit of Prime Minister Nehru, Mrs. Ghandi's father, to the United States in November 1961. Jackie was an effective, if unofficial, international diplomat. Prime Minister Nehru got along far better with Jackie than with Jack.

Below: Jackie, always the center of attention, is surrounded by government leaders and political dignitaries eager to have a word with her during a reception at The Elysée in France in 1961. Jackie's incredible charm and grace revitalized the White House and the American people. *Opposite:* On May 8, 1962, Jackie christened the USS Lafayette, a 7,000-ton (6,349t) nuclear-powered submarine, to great fanfare. Her popularity was at an all-time high.

A consummate hostess, Jackie made sure that every detail was carefully attended to and every guest was made to feel welcome. Pictured here in April 1962, Jackie warmly greets Nobel Prize winners at a dinner and reception hosted by her at the White House.

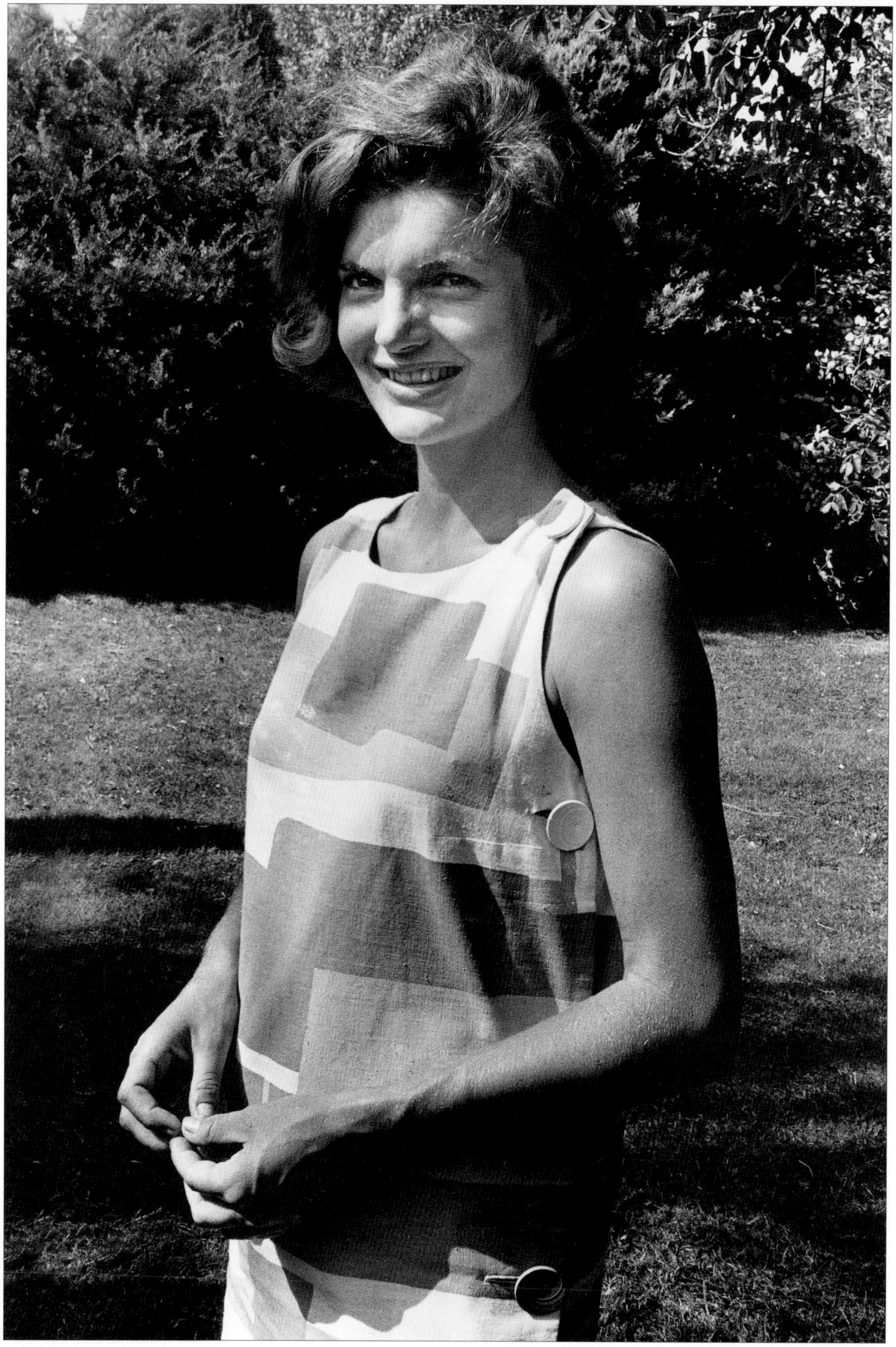

Though she was a profoundly private woman, Jackie understood that she—and, to some extent her family—belonged to the American people. Never unwillingly, but always with a hint of wariness, she would pose for the camera when necessary. Above: Though Jackie has dressed up Caroline and John, Jr., for the session, their natural exuberance shows the bond between a mother and her children. Opposite: In a casual moment at Hyannis Port, Jackie smiles for the photographer, but her sense of reserve is clear.

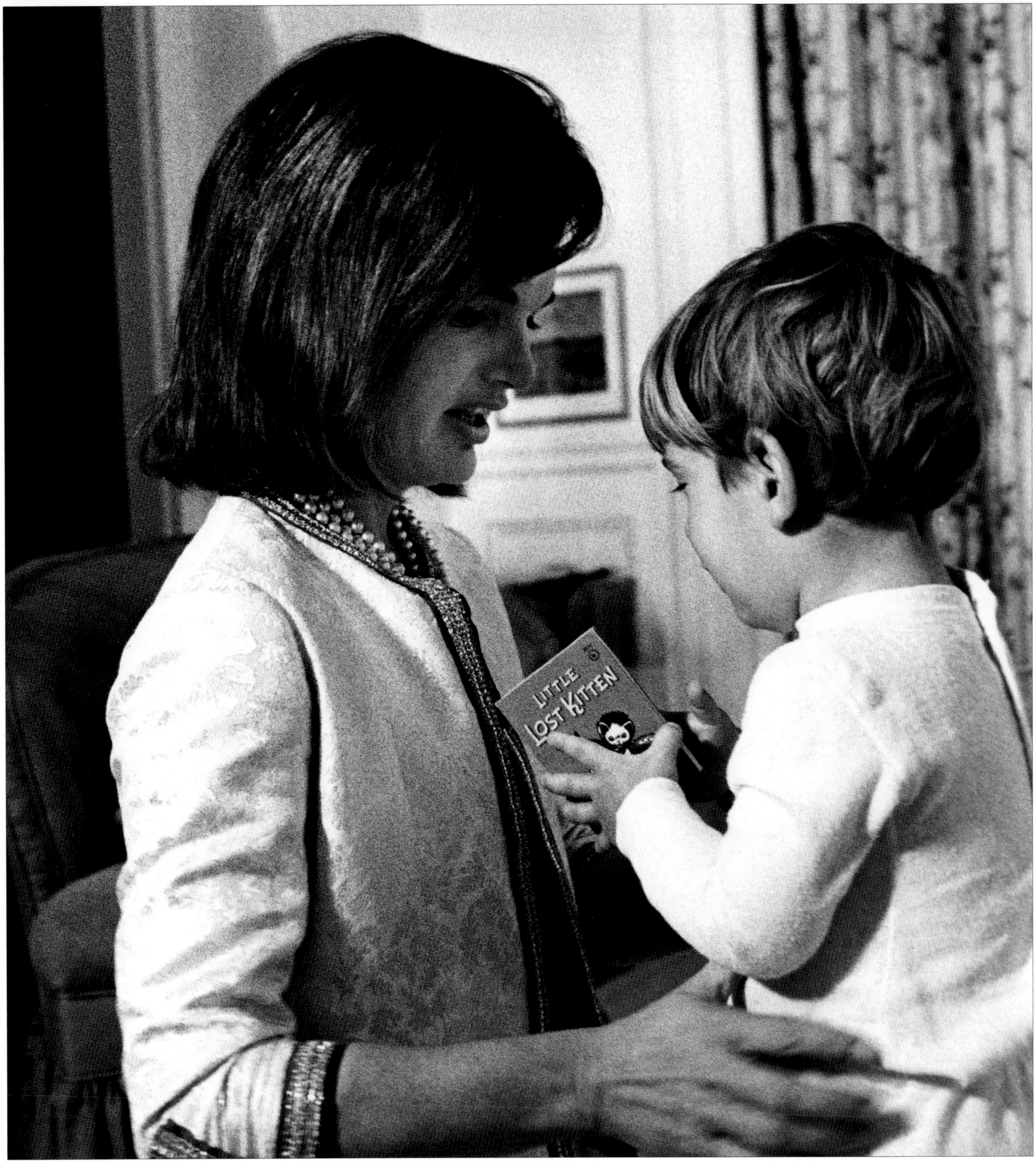
LITTLE
LOST KITTEN

Above: John F. Kennedy, Jr., nick-named John-John, was born shortly after John Kennedy won the presidential election in November 1960. Jackie nuzzles John-John's cheek in this photo taken by official White House photographer Cecil Stoughton in the White House nursery in August 1962. *Opposite:* Jackie was most at ease when she was with her children. Here, John-John shows his mother a book in the White House nursery in August 1962. *Pages 66-67:* Though Jackie tried to shield her children from photographers, keeping their appearances on camera to a minimum, she appears here with John-John as they delight in the children's pet canary in the White House nursery in 1962.

Above: A bit apprehensive about her trip, Jackie went to India in March 1962 on her first goodwill visit abroad unaccompanied by her husband. Opposite: "Hail, Jackie! Queen of America!" India poured their hearts out to Jackie who, escorted by Ambassador John Kenneth Galbraith, visited the Taj Mahal during her stay.

In Rome on March 12, 1962, Jackie visited the Vatican and met with Pope John XXIII to whom she gave a book of President Kennedy's speeches.

Below: Jackie is pictured here with her sister, Lee Radziwill, during her stay at Lee's summer home, Villa Episcopio, in southern Italy, in August 1962. Daughter Caroline also accompanied Jackie on the trip.

Above: Enjoying her summer vacation, Jackie sits at a "gelateria" in Ravello, Italy, in August 1962. *Opposite:* Jackie's striking beauty drew crowds every day during her summer stay in Italy.

Below: Jackie introduces Caroline to the delicacies of southern Italy.

Above: Jackie takes daughter Caroline and nephew Anthony swimming. While on holiday in Ravello, Jackie swam with Caroline and taught her how to water-ski. *Opposite:* Jackie and Caroline attend mass in Ravello's ancient cathedral.

Opposite: Jackie, wearing the pillbox hat she made famous, is about to greet the emperor of Ethiopia, Haile Selassie, on October 1, 1963. *Below:* President Kennedy, John-John, and Caroline greet Jackie as she returns from a trip to the Mediterranean and Morocco in October 1963. Bursting with excitement at their mother's return, the children run aboard the plane to greet her.

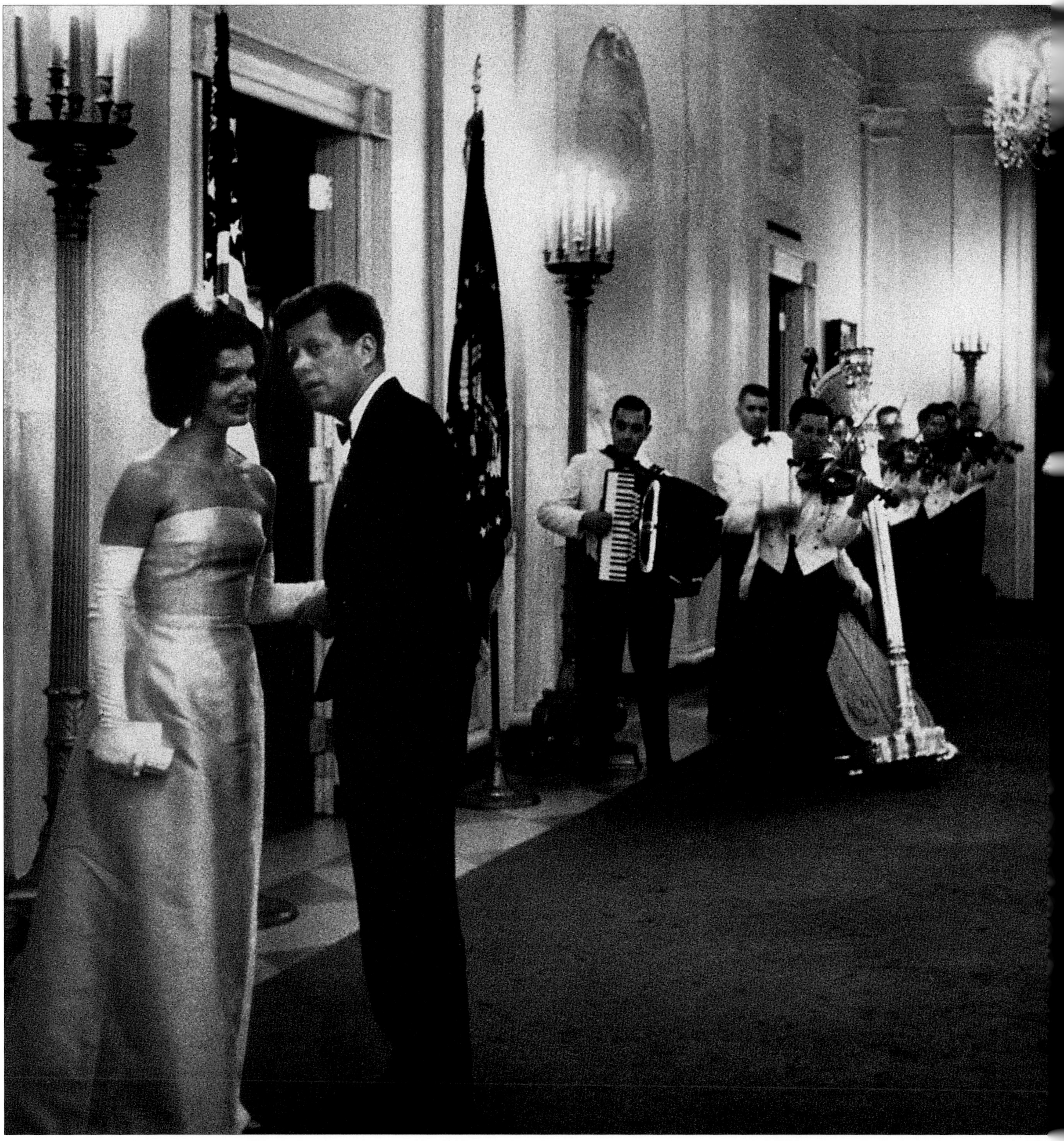

President and Mrs. Kennedy catch a quick moment together in the State Dining Room in 1963. Though Jackie often downplayed her influence, her views on politics and affairs of state were respected, admired, and often implemented by Jack.

80

Above: Jackie attends opening night of the Bolshoi Ballet at the Capitol Theater, in Washington, D.C., in 1963. Jackie adored the ballet and was a life-long supporter of the American Ballet Theater. *Opposite:* Jack and Jackie holding hands after Jack's address to the participants of the Campaign Conference for Democratic Women on May 22, 1962.

Jackie relaxes aboard the Honey Fitz. *She tried to heed her doctor's advice and avoid unnecessary stress during her pregnancy with Patrick in 1963. Sadly, Patrick was born prematurely and died shortly after birth.*

The eternal couple stand on the South Lawn of the White House, about to greet 1,700 children whom they invited to a performance of parades and marches by the Black Watch Royal Highland Regiment on November 13, 1963. Within a matter of weeks, Jack and Jackie would be separated by a tragedy that shocked the nation.

Opposite: At the funeral Jackie told her children, "We're going to say good-bye to Daddy, now." Here, she leads them down the steps of the White House as the president's body is taken to the rotunda in the Capitol. Below: A grieving Jackie holds tight to Caroline's and John-John's hands as the funeral procession for the slain president passes by. It is John-John's third birthday, November 25, 1963.

Above: Jackie and Bobby Kennedy revisit the president's gravesite at Arlington National Cemetery in Virginia on November 27, 1963.

Opposite: With Bobby by her side, Jackie receives the American flag from Jack's coffin. After the assassination, Bobby became a pillar of support for Jackie.

Opposite: Jackie is seated on the staircase of Joseph P. Kennedy's home in Hyannis Port awaiting her cue to appear on international television for a program celebrating JFK's birthday, May 29, 1964, when Jack would have turned forty-seven years old. *Below:* Looking windblown and lovely, Jackie arrives at Barnstable Airport in Cape Cod, Massachusetts, after having taped a television appearance in honor of her late husband's birthday.

89

Although she escaped the political pressures of Washington, D.C., by moving to New York City, Jackie could never have escaped the paparazzi. Here, Jackie manages to give a smile to the camera as she and her children enjoy an outing on the lake in New York City's Central Park in 1964.

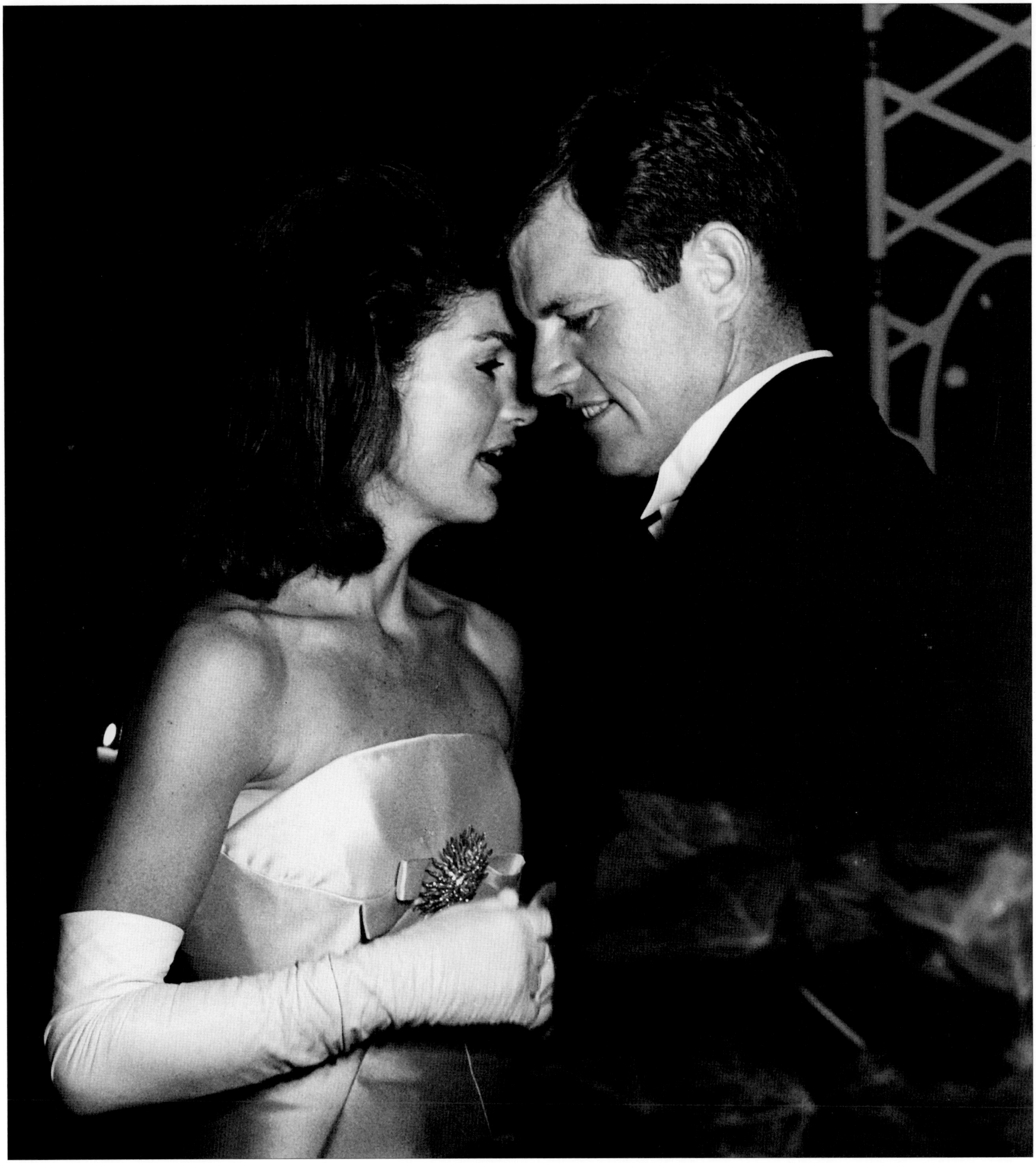

Above: Jackie surprises Bobby Kennedy as she darts from the sidelines to give him a kiss and words of support as he marches up Fifth Avenue during the St. Patrick's Day parade on March 17, 1966. *Opposite:* Jackie, looking elegant, with brother-in-law Ted Kennedy at a holiday gathering in December 1965. For three decades Jackie set trends and was a model of elegance and glamour for women around the world. *Pages 94-95:* On April 12, 1966, on holiday in Argentina, Jackie and Caroline look on as John-John proudly shows them his toy silver dagger. Jackie took great pleasure in her children. She was deeply devoted to them and was determined to give Caroline and John, Jr., as normal an upbringing as possible.

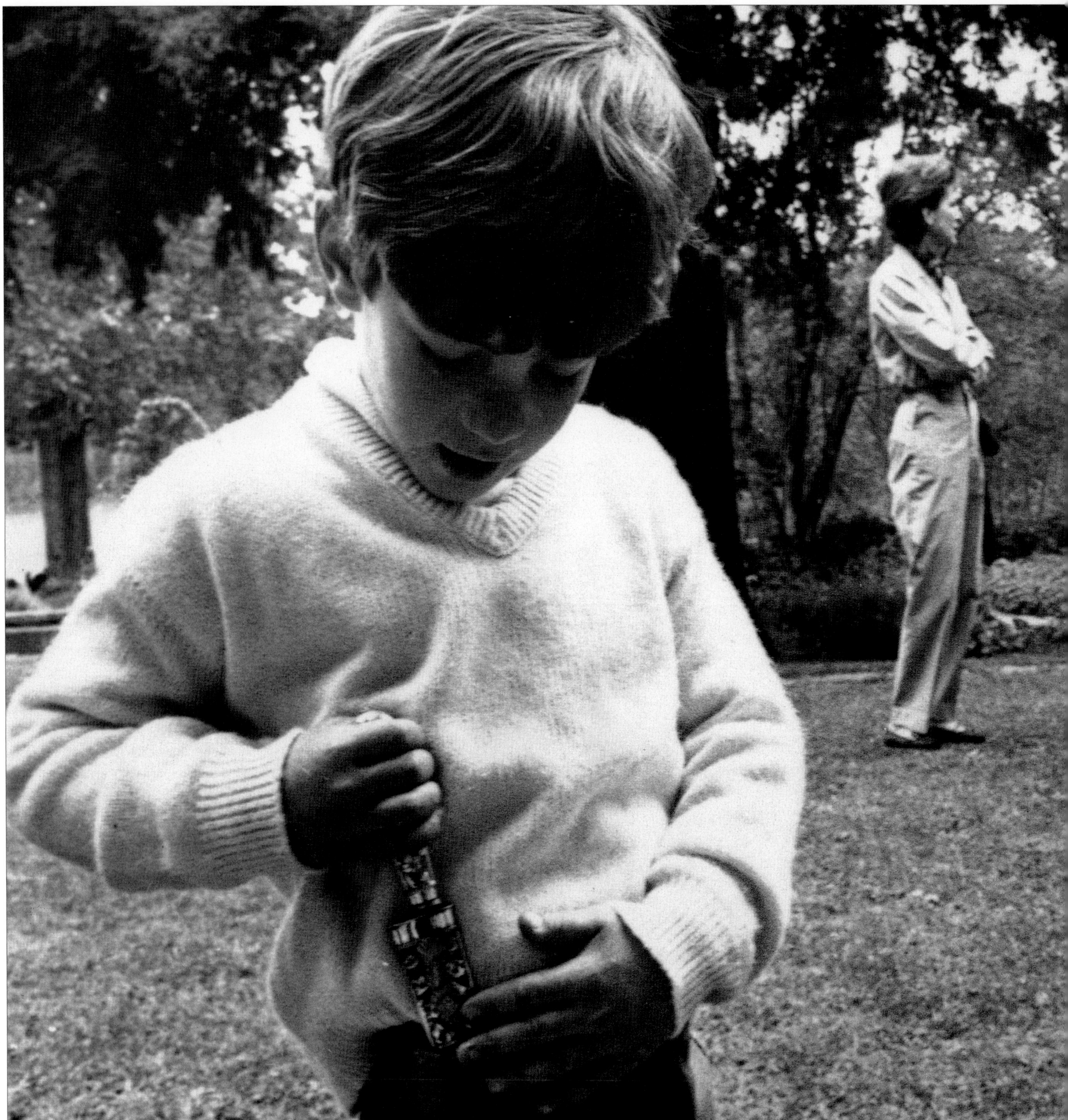

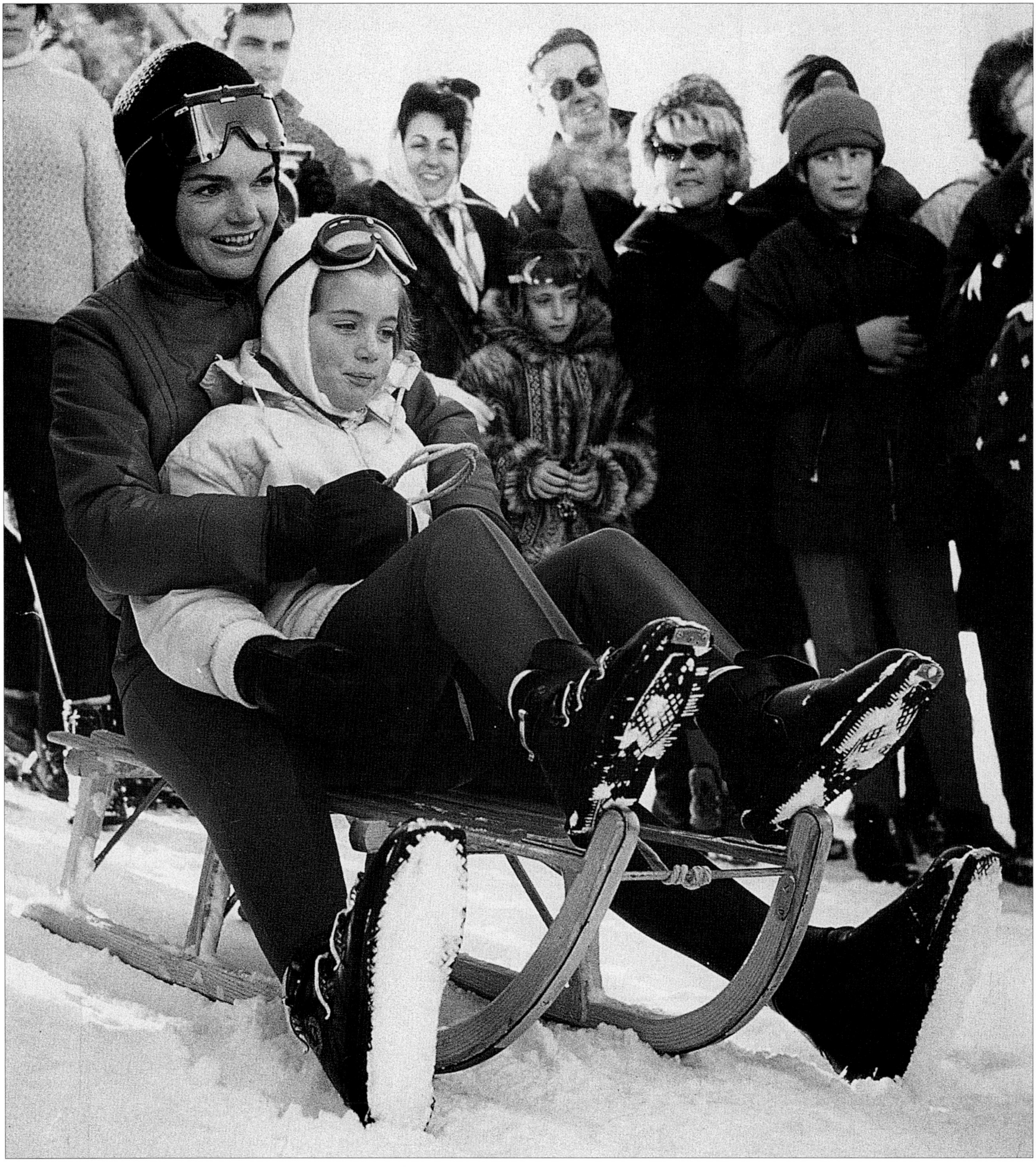

Opposite: Jackie and daughter Caroline are ready to go down a sledding hill during a vacation in Gstaad, Switzerland, in 1966. *Below:* Jackie passed on her love of sports and the outdoors to her children. Here, she and John, Jr., ride through the Irish countryside on horseback in the summer of 1967.

As little brother, John-John, and mother, Jackie, look on, Caroline christens the USS John F. Kennedy aircraft carrier in 1967.

Above: *Devastated by Bobby Kennedy's assassination, Jackie said, "We [Catholics] know death. . .if it weren't for the children, we'd welcome it." Here, she prays for Bobby in St. Patrick's Cathedral in New York City on June 7, 1968, the day before his funeral. Opposite: Jackie, Caroline, and John, Jr., kneel at the grave of Robert F. Kennedy, who was buried next to his brother President John F. Kennedy in Arlington National Cemetery, in August 1968.*

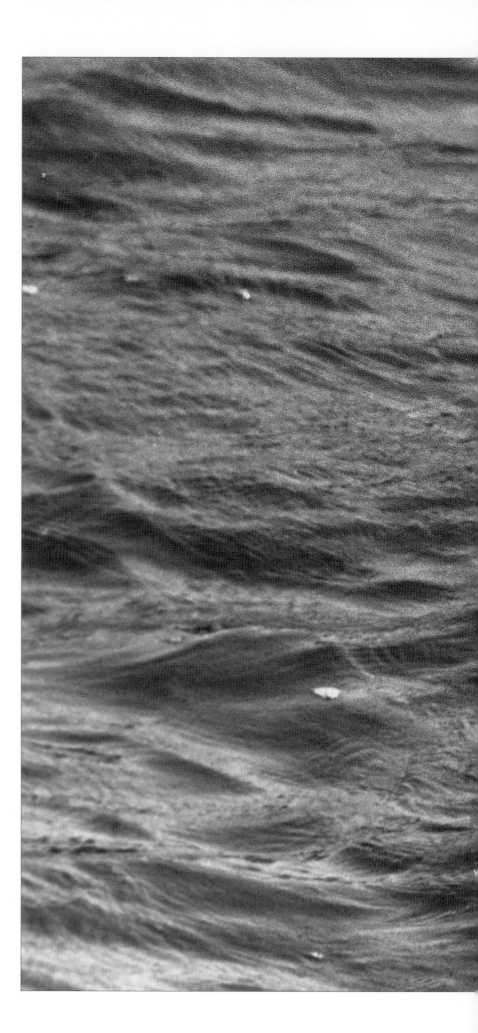

The water was always a favorite retreat for Jackie—whether she was swimming or sailing. Pictured here in October 1968, a week after her wedding to Aristotle Onassis, Jackie swims off the coast of Skorpios, the private island owned by her new husband.

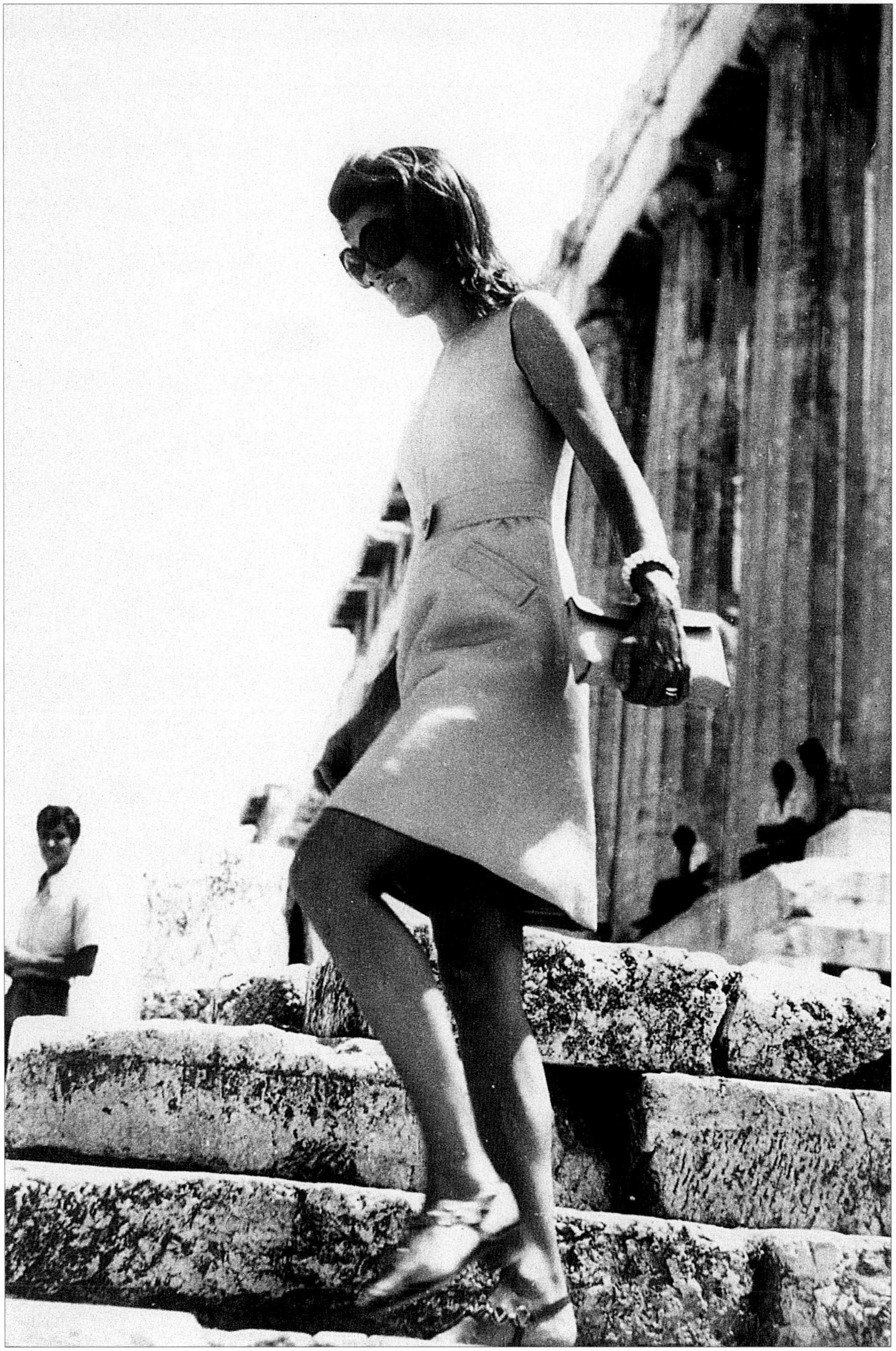

Above: Jackie, looking stylish, walks down the streets of Paris in 1969. She had the unique ability to make fashionable living look easy. *Opposite:* Jackie descends the steps of the Parthenon in August 1969. She was rumored to be pregnant at the time this photo was taken of her.

Above: Jackie and nine-year-old John, Jr., ride bicycles together, as they often did, through Central Park in New York City, November 1970. *Opposite:* Jackie enjoys some leisure time with Caroline and John, Jr. For Jackie, being a good mother was always the highest priority.

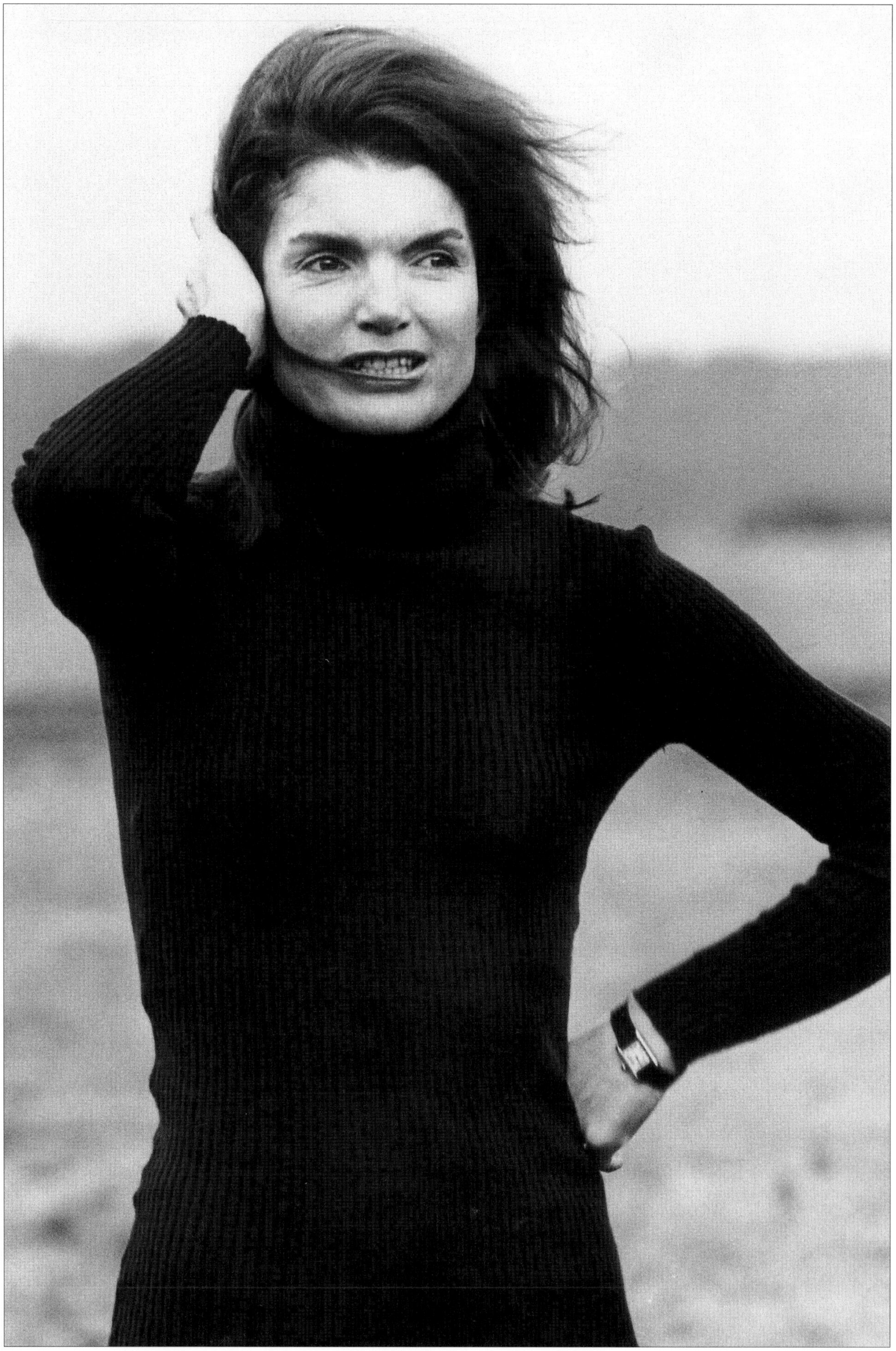

Opposite: As committed as she was to leading a private life, Jackie did not let the constant annoyance of the paparazzi deter her from pursuing her own interests and building her own career. Pictured here in 1969, she stops and allows a photographer to capture her in a moment of relaxation. *Below:* Jackie and Ari Onassis steal a quiet moment together to enjoy the sights during a ten-day tour of Egypt in March 1974.

Photographers flock around the generous patron of the arts as she leaves the theater after a night out on the town in New York City on May 11, 1970. Jackie flashes a radiant smile for the crowd.

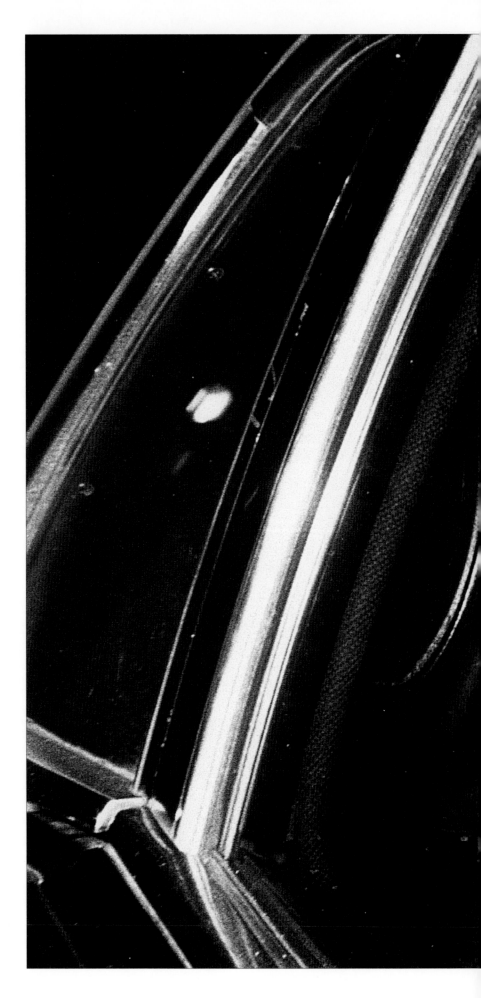

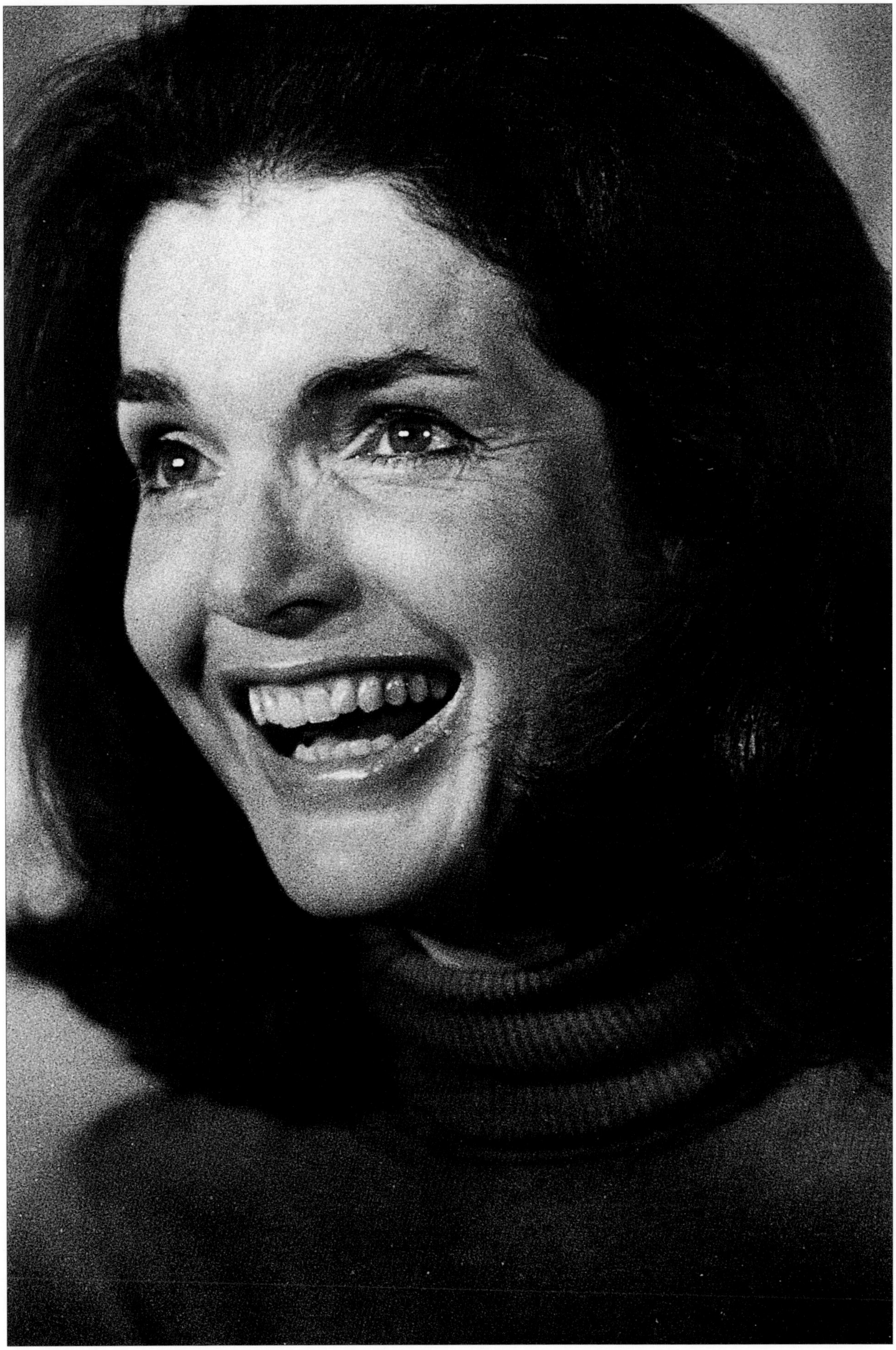

Opposite: In her later years, Jackie assumed her career as an editor with the characteristic blend of style and quiet determination that she had brought to all her earlier vocations. She is pictured here in a promotional photograph taken during her tenure as an editor at Viking Press, March 14, 1977. *Below*: Jackie Onassis and sister, Lee Radziwill, laugh as their group tries to make it to the car amidst the jostling of reporters and photographers trying to get a glimpse of Jackie O on May 15, 1970.

Above: *Jackie offers a child a sip of her orange juice during a walking tour of La Perla in Old San Juan, Puerto Rico, on March 11, 1980. She was there in support of her brother-in-law Senator Edward Kennedy, who was trying to secure the Democratic nomination for president.* *Opposite:* *Jackie embraces Ted Kennedy just after daughter Caroline's wedding to Edwin Schlossberg on July 19, 1986.*

Jackie was a deeply devoted mother and she treasured her role as a grandmother in her later years. She took a day off every week to spend with her grandchildren. Opposite: Grandmother Jackie and Rose, her first grandchild, born on June 25, 1988, have a chat in New York City's Central Park in 1992. Below: Here, Jackie calls to Rose and Rose's little brother, Jack, who stand atop a good climbing rock in Central Park.

Jackie is flanked by her children, Caroline and John, Jr., and brother-in-law Ted Kennedy at the ceremony presenting the 1992 John F. Kennedy Profile in Courage Award at the JFK Presidential Library in Boston on May 28, 1992. Profiles in Courage, *John F. Kennedy's Pulitzer Prize-winning book, bore the inscription, "This book would not have been possible without the encouragement, assistance, and criticisms offered from the very beginning by my wife, Jacqueline, whose help during all the days of my convalescence, I can never adequately acknowledge."*

Jackie speaks with President Bill Clinton at the rededication ceremony of the JFK Presidential Library in Boston, Massachusetts, on October 29, 1993.

Bibliography

Anderson, Christopher P. *Jackie After Jack: Portrait of a Lady.* Thorndike, Me.: Thorndike Press, 1998.

————. *Jack and Jackie: A Portrait of an American Marriage.* New York: William Morrow, 1996.

Anthony, Carl Sferrazza. *As We Remember Her: Jacqueline Kennedy Onassis, in the Word of Her Family and Friends.* New York: HarperCollins, 1997.

Dubois, Diana. *In Her Sister's Shadow: An Intimate Biography of Lee Radziwill.* Boston: Little Brown, 1995.

Heymann, C. David. *A Woman Named Jackie.* Secaucus, N.J.: Lyle Stuart, 1989.

Kennedy, John F. *The Quotable Kennedy*, ed. Alex J. Goldman. New York: Hippocrene Books, 1984.

Klein, Edward. *All Too Human: The Love Story of Jack and Jackie Kennedy.* New York: Pocket Books, 1996.

Koestenbaum, Wayne. *Jackie Under My Skin.* New York: Farrar, Straus & Giroux, 1995.

Ladowsky, Ellen. *Jacqueline Kennedy Onassis.* New York: Park Lane Press, 1997.

Onassis, Jacqueline Kennedy. *The Uncommon Wisdom of Jacqueline Kennedy Onassis: A Portrait in Her Own Words*, ed. Bill Adler. New York: Citadel Press, 1994.

Thayer, Mary Van Rensselaer. *Jacqueline Kennedy: The White House Years.* Boston: Little Brown, 1971.

Photo Credits

AP/Wide World Photos: pp. 102–103; ©Jacques Lowe: p. 37 left

Archive Photos: pp. 74, 75 right, 97, 104, 105, 107, 113; Alpha Blair: pp. 110–111; APA: p. 81; Archive France: pp. 58, 96; Express Newspapers: p. 108; The Morgan Collection: pp. 10, 22, 23; Popperfoto: pp. 86, 112

Camera Press/Retna Limited, U.S.A.: p. 75 left; ©Bachrach: p. 24; ©Jacques Lowe: pp. 9, 41, 46

Corbis: John F. Kennedy Library: p. 82

Corbis-Bettmann: p. 27

Everett Collection: pp. 90–91

FPG International: p. 73

Globe Photos, Inc.: pp. 7, 18, 28–29, 44–45, 55, 68, 80, 84, 98–99; National Archives: p. 63

IPOL, Inc.: pp. 72 both, 78–79

John F. Kennedy Library: pp. 2, 6, 11, 36, 37, 59, 60–61, 70–71; Harrington: pp. 32, 33, 34–35, endpapers; Jones: pp. 30–31; Rothstein: p. 85; Cecil Staughton: pp. 13, 64, 65, 66–67; Stanley Tretick: pp. 48–49, 56–57, 54

MacFadden/Corbis-Bettmann: p. 19

Photofest: pp. 8, 12, 50–51, 69, 88, 92, 94–95

Photofest/Icon Archives: p. 39

Retna Limited, U.S.A.: ©Jim Demetropoulos: p. 14

Reuters/Corbis-Bettmann: pp. 16, 118, 119

Rex U.S.A., Limited: p. 17; ©Keith Butler: pp. 116, 117

UPI/Corbis-Bettmann: pp. 20, 21, 25, 26, 37 right, 38 both, 40, 42, 43, 47, 50, 51, 52, 53, 62, 76, 77, 83, 87, 89, 93, 100, 101, 106, 109, 114, 115